This Body is an Empty Vessel

Poetry

Beaton Galafa

Edited by Tendai R. Mwanaka

Mwanaka Media and Publishing Pvt Ltd,
Chitungwiza Zimbabwe
*
Creativity, Wisdom and Beauty

Publisher: *Mmap*
Mwanaka Media and Publishing Pvt Ltd
24 Svosve Road, Zengeza 1
Chitungwiza Zimbabwe
mwanaka@yahoo.com
mwanaka13@gmail.com
https://www.mmapublishing.org
www.africanbookscollective.com/publishers/mwanaka-media-and-publishing
https://facebook.com/MwanakaMediaAndPublishing/

Distributed in and outside N. America by African Books Collective
orders@africanbookscollective.com
www.africanbookscollective.com

ISBN: 978-1-77925-572-3
EAN: 9781779255723

© Beaton Galafa 2021

DISCLAIMER
All views expressed in this publication are those of the author and do not necessarily reflect the views of *Mmap*.

Dedication

For my father

Born: September 2, 1937

Passed on: March 13, 2021

Acknowledgements

Some versions of these poems appear in a number of publications as follows:

Caustic Frolic: Cacophony

Bloom: Lingering Thought, Migraines, Empty Bodies

Necro Magazine Justice Issue #3: Echoes, Weed on the Seaside, Peril of Emptiness, Forgotten.

Human/Kind Journal: Bending Ways

"I Can't Breathe": A Poetic Anthology of Fresh Air: Broken

Kitchen Sink Magazine: Tombstone

Walking the Battlefield: Alone in a Cabin, Lunar Eclipse

Table of Contents

Foreword

Mankhokwe Namusanya

There would be three things that have always sought to mark Malawian poetry across the ages. Firstly, it is the political acerbity. Then, it is its firm rootedness in mythology. Of late, it has been its focus on performance. For the very latter, it is an interesting aspect because one struggles to place its origins. Is it that Malawi poetry is borrowing from global trends on the rise of spoken word poetry; or, maybe, it is borrowing from its vernacular variation? I might think both.

In this collection, however, Beaton Galafa introduces yet another dimension of Malawian poetry that has been sheltered under the weight of the familiar patterns that I have discussed above. Here is poetry that is personal yet spreading to have its tentacles struggling to grip into other equally slippery facets of life. In brief, Beaton writes his poetry to assuage his personal feelings yet in so doing he ends up massaging our shared experience – as Malawians, Africans and just as humans.

Beaton writes about his father, and mother – mostly his father. However, the narratives thereof of the two are not in any way dissimilar to those of the average person. In writing about his parents, he writes of loss as well as dreams deferred and even abandoned. This position then transcends beyond the personal aspect of the conversation. It becomes his, mine and ours. His poetry becomes pregnant with metaphors in which the position of those two important people in his life is replaced by other important people and things in our lives.

This collection opens with an abstract poem. It is, in a way, a foreshadow of what is to come through the entire collection. Much of the poetry that is served here is not built on the foundations of myths, stronger in their own regard. Rather, it is built on the strength of the human imagination. In one reading, this is the checked flow of a poet's consciousness; yet in another reading, this collection is the midnight musings and thoughts of a poet that haunts when the world is quiet and life wears a new ambiguous meaning. In so doing, that space of the personal is invaded by the impersonal – the strong defining feature of this poetry.

In *Mists*, he captures this reality as in a space of at least four lines; he blurs the lines between the personal and impersonal. In two lines, he writes of his father's dreams and ambitions; yet before we settle on that and dismiss it as fond memories of a besotted son towards his father, he brings on the table other illusions that most of us can share in: of politics. If in the rest of the work he has been attempting to portray the poetry as personal, here that portrayal is shattered as is 'the *revolution* that was branded a Swastika for the sole purpose of *plundering money*'.

Beaton has observed, learnt, and is growing in the Malawian poetry space. Thus, he also comes to the stage bearing the Malawian influence on his poetry. From the first identified feature of poetry from the centres of the world that have shaped his poetry, that of political acerbity, some of the poems in this collection come breathing that. It might not be fighting or mocking dictatorship that his poetry does, which was the tendency of the early Malawian poetry that saw poets detained. However, in reminding office holders of their promises or awakening the masses that politicians only care for themselves first and last, as he does in *Forgotten*, then his poetry betrays its influence. It is a strength that eludes most students and children of Malawian poetry.

His politics, however, is not fenced to the troubling reality of inter-country politics. It swells onto the bigger stage of historical and continental politics. There are questions on colonialism. There is satire on the same. He is cautious, though, knowing the state of the colonised and how they hang on to relics of colonisation. So, he does not breathe fire in his attack on the colonial vehicle of religion. He mutes his criticism, veiling it in poetic recollections of a period the average religious person would rather we not talk about. In *God*, he undoes a historical violence of colonialism and erasure.

As a Malawian, he cannot run away from myth even under the heavy assault of 'civilisation' and 'globalisation'. Myth certainly maintains human societies. In Malawi, it maintains, regulates and even demarcates the boundaries – especially in its poetry. In *Napolo*, he treks to the grave of one of Malawi's greatest poets, Steve Chimombo, to erect a shrine. He sings, and mourns, with Chimombo yet as a child of the realities that are both indigenous and foreign, he mourns further with the world and sings for it.

It is a disparate collection, with themes ranging across various questions the average African and citizen of the world asks on history, the future, hope and life. He does not offer solutions to any of the questions. However, where the answers are not provided, the thinking process is initiated. In this collection, there is poetry that is a product of thinking – as poetry is, or has to be – and it is poetry that invites you to do the same. If one is a fan of listening to performed poetry, then this is the book to get and read out aloud. Also, if one fancies quiet reading and meditation, here is a product you can enjoy.

For all of us whose interest is in the pulse and nature of poetry, understanding its mutations and progressions across the years, here is also a collection that stands at the confluence of time: belonging to the historical space of what would be Malawian poetry, occupying the space of what is Malawian poetry and eventually pouring into the future of what will be Malawian poetry which — for all practical purposes — must be global.

To the world, here is poetry that gives a feel of Malawi in the global village.

Inside a Dream

I am water

splashing

out of an empty vase

of flowers,

meandering inside

my veins disguised

as blood. I follow

the path of a worm

to some place inside

me dead & rotten. Its

powerful stench sterilizes

my thoughts as I try

to escape from cages

inside sad dreams

of my father & I in

imaginary conversations,

1

sometimes in hilly places

near government offices,

other times inside

lecture rooms

where he watches me

mould three chairs out

of clay to place in a grand

museum.

Rainbow

These colours

blind your eyes.

In between them

a fog keeps you

waiting for stars and the moon

to rocket out of the sky and diffuse

into streetlights of Lilongwe,

this place where dust & stench

from the city streams into

your lungs. In some nights

you're stuck alone in sewers

decomposing for a fresh start

underground when they find

you sad and rotten following

morning. The worst is when

three boys fish your eyes out

of their sockets as you float beneath

trash that flows southwards with

your empty soul to the lake.

Hypertension

What you don't see

coming is a mug cracking

i-n-t-o tiny bits that coffee

traps & scratches walls

of your narrow arteries with.

a doctor sits across you

staring at the back of your mind

to poke a ghost that hides

in bookshelves and pages

of a Malawian paper advertising

a job – side by side with posters

of men selling manhood enlargers.

this idea of something big

dangling between your legs

kills me when – locked

in nightmares – I must forego

everything and run for my life

if the doctor says

the emptiness inside me

is eating my heart slowly.

Blank Paper

No lines, no words,

imprisoned in the greyness

where I can hide my shame

and anger

for being abandoned in a

burning building. But what

was I thinking?

I saw your mother's body

covered in the mist

that morning, as we sat

waiting for meds with

tired drivers swerving

ambulances from side to side

evading holes that trapped

blood and skulls

when death demons

left their urns to roam these

crowded streets.

You may rush into the house

and borrow God's only book,

tear a page from the middle and

surrender your soul to Jesus.

I will be here staring

at the emptiness held hostage in

this blank page.

Empty Bodies

The hissing sound

of my voice

recorded from

a silver-grey phone

on oxygen

blocks a preacher's

noise as his saliva

& sweat from kids

running in these streets

hit the floor, waiting

for rains to flow together

into dying streams

where humanity

on empty tummies

pee & piss their grief

out, not knowing what

to offload from

empty bodies that

at times do not

even carry

homeless souls.

Footsteps

you can also

just fall from the sky,

plunge into a sea

of nightmares,

without wings, without

horns; a hollow space

wrapped in darkness.

yours is a wretched

body suspended in time

to rot and vaporise back

to heaven – this

time a destination

tucked between myths

of eternal hailstorms of fire

and the footsteps of a woman

echoing from a distance in a

narrow corridor leading you

back to everything

cold and still.

Reunion

Fridays are for a mother

and a son

to sit in the middle

of the road,

recreate

scenes from past lives

while a father's spirit

flutters at the edges of

the clouds.

A phone rings and the son

remembers a prayer

hiding in a motif of

a gospel song piercing

through the heart

when echoes of his father's

goodbyes and come-see-me

just-one-more-time

got louder, still lost

in the horns of a passing

truck.

Music

You will be a song

in a heart,

plucking nerves

like does the little bird

that breaks through

the window to stare at us

caged, but still charging forward.

the collection of whispers

filling this empty drum

is everything that separates you

from screams

as rivers swallow homes

and roads on their way to the ocean,

hiding in the silent woods,

away from time's ruthlessness

as it counts the tiny strands

of grey hair on your head.

you just sit there, an empty body

tucked under a canopy of vanity

sometimes humming,

sometimes pulling a string

from the guitar

deep inside your soul

as you travel to your past

in your father's footprints

in the sand.

I sit on the Clouds

the moon contains

the shadow of my father

trapped in its light.

i meet him before the night

catches the moon's patches

heading for collision

with a lost shooting star.

i sit on the clouds in the glory

of man's creation of day and night,

the flame in his soul cannot travel

beyond this web I tangle my feet in.

i promised my father

we would travel the galaxy

inside an empty pearl.

i am here

honouring a promise

again, i sit on the clouds

in the glory of mankind's imagination

waiting for the ray that carries

his spirit to bounce off

the clouds and fill the void

it carved out of my body.

i wasted our days

waiting

for

my

worth.

Cacophony

if i were you

i would not know what to choose too.

last night i slept well, my face stuck

into bits of wood

& felt your hand stretching onto a curtain

on toilet walls. i etched my nightmare

with a joke about little devils

on the fence outside our home startled

with the sun-ness of my wife & the cacophony

of two dogs growling with the winds.

i am a papyrus on a river bed, rotting

rooting for archaeologists & aqualungs

to rescue me from the timelessness of decrepitude.

tell my mother: i feast on moss & drink

from shells of a turtle that is stuck and

slowly drowning in a muddy plot of these

waters, with me.

A Quake in a Glass

what you saw

inside the cracks

of a glass:

a boy & a girl

ripping

each other's hearts

apart,

is not me.

i swallowed

an earthquake once

& gushed it out

one night

when lightning

& thunder

fought over who

reigned in a night

hidden in shadows

behind the mountains.

i can be in the glass

too, looking the spoon

in the eye,

stirring it,

& it – stirring me,

two to tango

as earth cracks open

to swallow

secrets of a troubled man

& the vomit of his saviour.

Weed on the Seaside

Between letters & the paper
lie a thousand seasons
of laughter to the first cry
& sorrow to the last breath.
I still see my father's hand
reaching out to touch my soul
for one last time.
now he rests on my thumbs
pestering foes as they threaten
to wash my fingertips in acid
& shovel logs down my throat
to stop my big mouth
from gushing secrets
they vow never to listen to.
I am a weed in this season of
hysteria – they are all drowning

in stories of fire & thunder

engulfing the enemy's kingdom

until the sea vomits them back

& they wake up on my thumbs,

my father & I still pestering them.

Forgotten

my fingertips rebel

& run after the paper

one after another

they rip into shreds

modern books of history

crammed with

hysteria of a revolution

like we never danced

before the dogs

came barking

and tore us into tiny bits

one after the other

swallowed by earth

or prison walls

to the bone.

Mother

is the sound

of birds

with whispers of wind

doused in cries of angels

& lullabies of demons

standing frozen,

trapped in a dying house

that never really lived.

were I not these metal

scraps searching for

beggars to pick & caress

me, my mother

swam across a river

& gold wetted

her from toe to head,

we would be dining

with kings & queens,

our tables tucked beneath

the lining in your eye bags.

At sea

Feel the heart of my soul

& tell me,

if it also feels

the texture of your palm, or

the lost paths which crisscross

at the centre,

floating like your

spirit in a raging sea.

my father wanders in the wind

thinking about where in the waters

we can swim together,

the storm swerving us back & forth,

a tug of war between many pairs:

fire & water; life & death; peace &

war.

mother thinks there's nothing

anyone can do to melt the iceberg

& let our worn-out bodies

wash to the other side of the sea.

the moon thinks otherwise,

it will carry our shadows

over to the future.

in return we will water its surface

to wash away dirt and blood

in the footprints of Neil Armstrong.

Father

Some day in 1937…

father is a blue cotton cloud

hanging low.

he stares at the sea

from the centre of a tiny dot

where a crown rests

waiting for us to rise

in smoke & vapour

for his coronation

and salvation of

our tattered souls.

2nd September…

i want

to explore the grave

and talk to his heap

of bones – if they can

connect us to let him know

i miss the photo of an old man

shining in greyness

on the veranda of his home,

sometimes a stick in hand,

sometimes a straight back

standing on a rung of bricks

that is breaking away

after seasons of rains and

the pain of a fallible body.

13th March...

i sit on the same

veranda staring at people

come and go with my father

leading the procession.

his queen looks straight

into the eyes of the night

as screams of little ones

die in the whispering

winds of 2020.

Mists

In the mists

father still whispers

to me.

he would be a lawyer

given a chance.

he did not hear

how they mounted a putsch

branded it a revolution

with a swastika

and plundered all the money.

i am the face you see

in the coins and notes

surviving nausea from

stench in their trousers

as they vomit the little demons

they drink and eat at *Bwandilo*.

What scares you more,

demons or their sender?

these little devils can rebel

and devour you along with

the money you looted

but the devil scares me more

when the mists are gone

and father is not looking.

Out of Nothing

between

the shower and

a cup of coffee

is a man who thinks

this whole universe

spurted itself out of

nothingness.

when ghosts lurk

in his courtyard

he recoils to the one

dark corner carefully

sprayed with insecticides

and a small dose of

holy water

stolen from earth's

sweating glands

in mornings and midnight.

he reimagines

his frame

stripped off flesh – this

very earth spurted

out of nothingness –

turning and turning

alone in rotting

wood as voices

that once professed

love for him fade

into a silent night.

God

a man thinks:

my body was torn

out of history pages.

these same stories

of purges and believers

crawling in sewers

shred my heart into

tiny bits I scatter

on land and sea

to discover truth

rolled out on

papyrus reeds or hidden

in strokes carved out of

trees and rocks until I

meet your father who

blindfolds me in a fog

and asks how I think

it could've been

possible that ape man

sinned out dark chocolate

and God rolled our

bones in it with a mark

on the forehead

so our hunters

wouldn't miss us even

in dark sitting rooms

of our silent homes

when drunkards sent

distress calls in the streets

of America.

we shouldn't have given

the creator an option.

we too would be on

ships and planes

preaching salvation

as our police gagged

their own people and

sprayed bullets on

their backs.

In the Stream

Father introduces
himself to my professor
and extends his hand.
he smiles and embraces
his charm, they whisper
to each other when I come
to hold his hand and leave.
sometimes all I see
is him lying on the hospital
bed wondering whether
I could have done more.
take him to the stream,
for example,
strip off my clothes
and let him laugh his
lungs out if he could

as I battled my way through

his memories of a time

he could not even dream of

my existence, as his feet ran

from the scorching sun

finding refuge in the stream's

running waters

so he could forget the pain

of his frail body struggling

to hold on to an escaping

soul.

Empty Vessel

no soul, no flesh

just a hollowness

punctuated with broken bones,

marrows sucked up

by fatherless spirits

wandering in the streets

of barren earth.

it is a vessel: sirens and

gunshots gnawing at my nerves,

midnight i see a man & a woman

tussling for the emptiness.

whichever way the winds blow

i follow. i am a carcass with

a name & a family to mourn

when what remains of my stump

melts in a volcano, lost

in equatorial rain forests

where i lie side by side with

flesh & bones from timeless seasons

of pain & loss.

Broken Leg

My life

is a broken leg

watching me attempting

to jump from upper

stories of a furnaced house.

i save this pain for the last.

i will be on a toilet seat

thinking i am squatting

in a latrine, praying that

as i pass the pain and grief

out, winds do not blow off

the roof or push me in to

swim with maggots and

swallow stench from this

mass grave. emptying

your bladder after a night

of swallowing poison is

liberating. you tiptoe

to the window

to welcome the sun

as it rises for another

miserable day in the life

of a ghost.

Blown Away

at the blow of every wind

i feel the searing of my body

the skin erodes into dust

and flies away

its particles landing on

dry surfaces of leaves

in a neighbourhood bush.

if i should go, i will rise

in smoke and follow rays

of sunshine to the centre of

the sun. with wide streets

filled with nothing

inside me, i can neither melt

nor burn. i will be bringing

my heap of dust with me

where father and i can tap

some clay & water to breathe

life into a new effigy of

the creator.

Tombstone

The pile of stones

you see on a dull path

through the wall into

empty streets

is a tombstone

for a body

that wandered off

to the earth's laterals

and fell into a well

carving emptiness

in this corpse housing

an exhausted spirit.

Footsteps in the rains

The sound of music

in the rains,

and footsteps

washed in songs

of birds

attempt to fill

the emptiness

of my body

as i lie on bed

motion-less

like a man without

a soul must do

before elders

come to dispatch

his wearied stump

to the forests,

under one concrete block.

Lingering thought

i am an incomplete poem

rolling

to fill the void

grief carves out of

a book page. the grass

and a pile of dead leaves

burning behind my home

speak to the spirits of

my ancestors as they stand

in the night watching

smoke wandering off

to all sides of the earth

in all seasons. they remember

me bending my back

for hours tussling for turf

with leaves from a dying

autumn. without hope,

without sorrow. just

lost in thoughts of

everything about everything

not noticing how trees

survive all seasons to

bear testimony of

winds and fires and rains

that travel through leaving

destruction behind. i am a

poem in writing

rolling itself out to understand

how grief is constant

even with time, always

tucked beneath our eyes

to drop into an expansive sea of

tears any time of the year.

Migraines

A deflated body

tossed in mud &

dirty streams

floats side by side

with garbage,

there must come a time

now or in the sweeping of years

when it will stick

to the bottom

& rest.

but that is just that.

migraines will not just

go as they came

until the cavity

in your hugs is filled

with butterflies & flowers

unmanned by strangers

in the twinning of our

sorry lives.

Napolo[1]

All that flows

is water escaping

to the sea. There is

a hole trapping

raindrops at the foot

of the mountain, letting

them off in an orchestrated swoop

to come our way and narrate

to our kids stories of

huge serpents spitting fire

under the current of

violent waters sweeping

through streets in and outside

---

[1] In Malawian mythology, *Napolo* is a serpent that lives under mountains and causes floods. Malawian poet Steve Chimombo used the mythology as inspiration for some of his poems.

our hearts. When the sun rises,

it will find your home floating

like Arab corpses rejected by

the Indian Ocean in liberation wars.

A Cup of Coffee

I sip from a burning mug

and sit back.

the roof inside my mouth

crumbles, burying

letters before

they escape the tip of

my tongue to the laterals

on the sides of my lips.

I need a man holding a camera

to follow me into the other

dimension and capture

hope escaping the loneliness

of my heart, moulded from

the moment I saw my father's

soul slipping off my mother's

hands on a dirty hospital bed.

Memory

Memory is a crushed skull

atop a worn out corpse lying still

in the drains of a street blocked

with burning tires and bricks and stones

from jubilant rioters.

It is the rotting body of a woman

buried in the middle of nowhere

by a loving husband who breaks

her windpipe to flee her from

enslavement of poisonous gases

spurted out of car manufacturers

in the first world.

There is a young boy gasping for air

in cells of the secret police with ribs

and the cavity open to let his heart out

to the regime as he did in the streets

before his bricks met boots

and guns and a heavy pounding

that calmed him to sleep

before waking up again

in these dungeons

– and again transcending through smoke

to sit on clouds and ride stars

discussing with God about a small dot

in the middle of nowhere

perpetually burning from greed.

It is a chain of hills towering

over burning shacks in which mothers and

daughters hide in day and night from

fathers and sons and brothers and uncles

of other mothers and daughters trying

to crush them between life and death

when their maker turns the other side

to spy on worlds that really matter.

this one can burn

and rot and wash away to the oceans.

There is a dark hollow cave with echoes

of bats flip-flapping

and rats running around from one corner

to the other in an endless corridor that smells

like the rooms we were packed in

when our granny broke her leg and

they said it had to be tied to the rock

under their watch because

there was nothing they could do

in this dog eat dog world.

It is a brother on oxygen wondering why

he couldn't even be allowed to say goodbye

to his sons and daughters and

fathers and mothers and wife

when all he had known was loyalty to the gods

while he roamed the earth.

My memory is one long night of sleep.

Revolt

The sun has revolted.

Its nose sniffs water

out of our barren

lands as we keep staring

at vapour rising from

lakes

leaving cracks that keep

their mouths open

in dry mud hoping for

equatorial rains

to rush their floods

down and save us

from this fury.

Not even the moon cares.

The night sticks its nose

out sneezing and shooting stars

as our kids stand

in the open ground

engulfed by darkness

pointing at glittering rocks

rolled down

by rioting angels

to curve craters out

of this forsaken earth

and trap us in

until we return

to righteousness.

The humid air connives

with winds to breathe fire.

Reminiscent of old days

when dragons and dinosaurs

roamed this side freely.

we stayed in heavens scared

of both until God thought it

wise to replace the latter with

our sorry selves when we

surprised him and outlived

the dragon's breathe.

Four men just fell yesterday.

I felt my heart move closer

to the grave where my brothers

hold hands looking over us.

I looked for winds that were

naïve and promising

that I would run around

in the streets and tell everyone

resurrection happened again

in the land of fire

but the cock crowed

and the dog barked

and I was out again

chasing thieves

and dreams.

Days piling on days and

months on months

unmask brutes that wander

around hunting stars

in the galaxy until they stumble

on gemstones and your heart

shreds again.

Like the afternoon

it watched you

stare at the vapour rising.

Like the night

it watched your kids

stare at the meteorite in the dark.

Like the day it saw your heart

tear when lava melted your soul.

Wine & Whiskey

My voice is lost

in whispers of winds

and the pulse of my heart

as the night and its screams

from bars and clubs

hold my soul against

resting calmly

on a bed that does not belong

to any of my body parts.

I float in the loud screams

of dogs – homeless, stateless -

just like me and

the wrinkled scalp

tucked under

my unkemptness

staring at the galaxy

from the corner of my mind.

I pity the world's loneliness.

I smile at the single drop

of dawn's dew

that keeps me company

in the thick web of nothing

where I have no heart you could

tear apart

if you had opted for solitude

engulfing our whole universe

while you were gone –

drowned in

wine and whiskey

our fathers lost land

to the gods for.

You may toss me

to the back of your mind

where I will wrestle

with dirt and contempt

and death until

earth overpowers me

or

hang me loose from your mind

so when I fall I must crack

a rib and break my neck

as you wait for the rains

to wash me away into drains

where kids will piss and poop

on me until I can no longer

smell myself.

Either way

I am a hero to the tiny bits of wood

I call my heart burning in flames,

its screams heard to itself

and my father

and mother as they sit on the veranda

of an old home

forever waiting to see

the shining faces of my family.

I Despise Your Heroes

This country will explode.

I sit here craning my neck

into the future

I want to explode along with it.

Wherever it will go, I will.

I listen carefully to the wind

As it whizzes past

after long sunny days.

It does not bring any news

but exports our calamities

to the sea where pirates

hijack it and rip into shreds

papers on which stand

our burning fields

and what remains of us

is the story of a baby with

broken legs in need of crutches

and a tear in the eye

of a sympathizer passing laws

in faraway lands.

Your heroes cling to kites and fly

around, stand on podiums

lobbying in empty rooms

and spit their throats out

to report fires they ignite

as they tussle with deadlines

of projects we take bullets

and raze homes for.

Every night my soul slips out

and stares from the moon

at the cycle recurring

in hot currents as hyenas

(mis)lead dogs away into the night

sweeping streets clean for a pack

of wolves to walk over and

thank God there were

no churches to teach man how

to live within the reason

of another.

And just like that, I sit

all night long waiting to explode

– just like everyone else.

Morgue Attendant

take note of the time,

after some hours we will

want to release this body.

who was he to you?

is. he is. what remains

after earth stole from us

last night. first his voice

then his frail body

sweating as death sucked

the remaining heat out

to let my mother's hand

resting calmly on his forehead

freeze with grief as i tried

acting brave, with sorrow

eating away my heart

bit by bit remembering

how i could not stand up

for him when the monster

opened its mouth. we all saw it

crawling into the sitting room

of our home he called a museum

until yesterday when father

decided to take commands direct

from our maker.

Dusted

The sun is travelling

westwards. That, is a sign

of an approaching night

that plans to absorb you

in its eternal darkness.

This night reeks of rot

that I don't want to stare

at my heart ripped into

shreds by loss travelling

on a rail line that cuts

through mountains and

penetrates the ocean

to touch souls of families

floating to Europe before

their heads hit a rock

and they swim to its bed

to spend a night or two

    waiting for the coastguard.

Bending Ways

the man

in the mirror

is staring at the dirt on my nose.

i lift my arm to wipe the dust

off its face.

it laughs and coughs

into my lungs where its particles

shred into tiny threads

the little heart I borrowed

from the sun when gods melted gold

and wove them into a mass of blackness

floating on all seas and oceans of the universe.

we're all living on borrowed time.

earth must bend its ways to let us flow

in its streets crowded with bows and arrows

travelling through the flesh of our souls

as we bend on our knees to let monsters

know we're choking.

Broken

Power

Is not my brother

In a tear dropping down

To the bottom of a glass

With cracks in its base.

I tear off pages from a book of life

And chew them like gum

They swallow the spit alive,

Sit on the fence listening to my dry throat

The coughs go as they come

The voice tumbles to the bottom of the river

I cross with the rain waters up my waist

Rooting for my death.

A log misses me as it rolls in mud

With father's ghost washed from the grave.

A clog catches me and twists my bones,

Fits me into the earth's narrower spaces.

Broken, I lie on my back listening to myself

Gasp like my father on a tired hospital bed.

My breath satisfies the soul of his knee

Resting calmly on the neck of my history.

Peril of Emptiness

I spend my time

in front of an imaginary table

gathering escaped words

into knives & arrows

to cut through dumbness

of these candid nights

where we sit and feast

on fantasies & hallucinations

of uprightness.

perhaps if we were honest

with the letters,

if we had explained

to them the peril

of emptiness

in our brain cages,

they could have stayed

easily

knowing how ink

fades away

when

soaked

in water.

that way our memories would have stuck

to the greyness of prison walls forever.

Sun in the Desert

i want to walk out of my house,

feel the softness of wind blowing

its coldness into my lungs

and laugh at the sun which hangs

from a distance, shivering. but

darkness scares me. i am rethinking

the idea of plucking feathers off

this turkey on a winter morning.

night wrestled away my father

by tricking us into sleep or looking

the other way. i am always scared

of melting my bones or burning my

flesh if i go out on any sunny day.

how many suns does the desert

have that everyone who pierces

its heart turns into sand before

the seas and oceans even have

the chance to take their pound of flesh?

Locked Up

One, two, ten, fourteen
When I'm done with the numbers
I will stand on the banks of *Shire*
To listen to the water
As it mingles with nothingness
Zigzagging around ferns and mosses
In the bright days of my life.
Earth has wrestled away everything from me
Drained the waters our fishermen paddle on
Burnt the bushes our hunters run through
Dug the roads our cars ram into each other on
Frozen the arms we hold on a night out
Placed a hill between my heart
And my mother's
Without a hole drilled through
For her aroma to travel through

Unravelling all patterns of survival

And stick just beneath my nose

So I can scare away the solitude

In the greyness of my days

Caged in this cell

Where I have to sit all day praying

To the luck of civilization to send a mole

And pull me out when the pandemic

Is not watching.

Prodigal

Death

by

ulcers

or

death

by

pneumonia. I choose to run to the mountain

where none will find a body whose lungs to tear apart

and throw the patches into acid or whose stomach to burn

when stress and pepper chain me to the walls of doom.

I will wander freely hanging in the air far from heaven

and far from the pangs of man and his strange pandemic.

I want to write man's history again when the disease is gone

I want the next black man to sit at the shores of Lake Malawi

and reminisce on a past he will only live through the calamities

that befell us when we were not watching, and bats and labs

went to war over who really had to reign – West or East.

Fated

This idea is a playing field

Its brains spattered in drains

Along with mud and dirt

Our faith is in fate's compassion

If it wishes to let us live

We will survive.

Woman

Now that you are here,

every path leads to you,

like a million statues of gold

hanging on walls and sitting

on floors in mountain temples,

a mother with a circle of yellowness

from the sun painted around the head

carrying a baby on her laps,

an image of emptiness lurking

in the back of our heads,

& a template of the words

they arranged us into when they set

rules to restrict vagabonds.

you entwine my soul with the oily

strands of your braids' blackness.

we must create our own world &

let your womb birth black gods

to free our ancestors from chains

of slavery they gag our genes with

as earth ages out of our narratives.

Echoes

I sit

& stare at the wall.

it stares back

its greyness

eating the emptiness

of my soul.

the water drops

a melody

into the sea

whispering

to ghosts,

their rotten flesh

tangled

with bones of

the wood pirates

dragged

across the Sahara.

there is neither night

nor light

on the other side

of the sea.

echoes

of cries

& windscreens shattered

rise together into the clouds

to rinse heaven of the dirt

of man

& let our spirits dangle,

hanging

from

webs

of

spiders,

woven

from

tales

of

life.

Raindrops

when i think of souls

loneliness freed from prison walls

in its days of power,

the idea of caves to lock

human freedoms and free will in

scares me.

i am imagining *Anjiru* whispering

to his mother about drilling a hole

into the dirty grizzly walls

through which to run to the world

where bodies pile in the streets

and lies about them wander from lip

to lip waiting in queues for a hug.

who's there to ask about plagues

that rained on us several seasons

ago when gods were finally done

with us?

today everyone sits at the edges

of the clouds pouring tears into

raindrops to wash our sins along

with the pandemic away to the

earth's laterals where they will

fall off into the cavities of history.

Void

Inside this song

i hear things.

my mother split her

heart among us,

dust from my father's corpse

filled the insatiable well.

we will listen to the winds

howling about creatures

with birds perching

on each other's back rising into horns.

such bravery, dad crawls past monsters

& mum performs lullabies to trap nights

in our eyes.

i refuse to hide in dreams,

all alone in darkness,

i do not know how nothingness

paddled its way up from the earth's laterals

to claim half of my life every time

the man in my dreams tries to escape

into the abyss of happiness that is me.

this world is not the shadow

he sees off the waterfalls under the deception

of moonlight.

On a Winter Morning

In the city when it snows

we clean our souls with

a hot shower,

hide the ruggedness of our feet

in winter boots,

enclose the fingers in gloves,

& meander under

& within

an electric blanket

& a life.

but the coin has two sides.

the other

has a frozen body discovered on a road passing through mountains.

Heroes

I've stopped counting.

days, months, years…

matter to those whose

palms stay greased

with milk & honey

in all the many moons

you freeze in the night

with a soul in tatters

wondering how the

heart wraps itself in

bandages all seasons

of its life.

You cannot stop

counting your broken

fingers. What do you

remember of your

father & your mother

the night they learnt

you were going to moult.

Stop right there.

how did they even live

& love in the tumults of

sand dunes & desert storms

when all they had was

each to the other

If I should live again,

lend me the eagle's eye

from my first cry

to the day mother stops

me from running to the river

to talk to the gods secretly

again when I should be

helping her hold on

to the soul of my father

trying to rip her heart

into shreds.

Last moments

I am reliving our last moments

with a man i met on a peak

after sliding and rolling

down the mountain

a few times.

he stammers as he tries to joke

about things i cannot remember.

i look at his hair, its greyness

reminding me of the emptiness

time creates as pillars vanish

with mists in the morning

when our swollen faces

can no longer hide themselves

away. we sit on that single

mango tree through which

whose branches we watched

the sun set, sometimes

a dog wagging its tail on your feet,

as we discuss life and show each

other the loneliness of the world

with grandmothers limping

around in empty fields

searching for survival.

Deception

I am done with the noise of

Broken windows

Scattered glasses piercing wounds

Of loneliness

Carved out of my flesh

By runaway soldiers

Lost in unquenchable thirst for power

And revenge.

I smell the tires and flesh burning

On the road and the thug's waist

Jurors flipping papers

Pointing to where winds must blow

Along with the blood and jubilation

Of a fire raging through and through

Cars overturning on our coffin lids

Connecting us to our pauperism

On this long march to deception.

Everyone to Their God

For me

That grey-haired hill

Stashed with light in the dark

For ages

Welcoming my wearied bits

As I carry my present into

Your soft arms wriggled with

Seasons of life and death

Dust falling off my head

To cleanse the tips of my strands

Of dreadlocks and the empty field of

Plainness, off which the light in your eyes

Bounces

Is the vessel through which I shall travel

To the past and

Witness the night

God spurted us out of
Nothingness.

Alone in a cabin

To say I will die

You don't scare me.

I don't remember living.

As I've trudged up the stairs of life

Leaping from second to second

I've seen mankind live through fire and ice

Charred flesh in flames and blood frozen cold

Screams falling silent and teeth biting frost

Yet, when the ice melts and the leaves fall

I've seen the sun and the moon tussle over

Our bliss when the thorny crown resigns to fate.

Lunar Eclipse

in the moon's worst days

I belong to its brightest side

coiled in the night

it never shows to earth.

this disease-ridden earth.

in the darkest of hours,

I sit at the laterals

staring at humanity as its soul

trapped in dust and coughs hangs on

to threads of hope on the moon's rays

bouncing off the lakes and rivers.

everything we birthed races towards death.

the sadness and joy are the stars

that brighten the skies

you float on when you lie

on the floor reminiscing when

you were at war with the gods

and science said

you were just hallucinating again.

in the moon's worst days

my soul languishes in loneliness

but I do not despair

because listening to the night as it canvasses hope

for civilization when dawn takes over

I hear summer rains whispering

from a distance – rushing

to rinse the streets

of gloom

and

doom.

Mmap New African Poets Series

If you have enjoyed *This Body is an Empty Vessel* consider these other fine books in **New African Poets Series** from *Mwanaka Media and Publishing:*

I Threw a Star in a Wine Glass by Fethi Sassi
Best New African Poets 2017 Anthology by Tendai R Mwanaka and Daniel Da Purificacao
Logbook Written by a Drifter by Tendai Rinos Mwanaka
Mad Bob Republic: Bloodlines, Bile and a Crying Child by Tendai Rinos Mwanaka
Zimbolicious Poetry Vol 1 by Tendai R Mwanaka and Edward Dzonze
Zimbolicious: An Anthology of Zimbabwean Literature and Arts, Vol 3 by Tendai Mwanaka
Under The Steel Yoke by Jabulani Mzinyathi
Fly in a Beehive by Thato Tshukudu
Bounding for Light by Richard Mbuthia
Sentiments by Jackson Matimba
Best New African Poets 2018 Anthology by Tendai R Mwanaka and Nsah Mala
Words That Matter by Gerry Sikazwe
The Ungendered by Delia Watterson
Ghetto Symphony by Mandla Mavolwane
Sky for a Foreign Bird by Fethi Sassi
A Portrait of Defiance by Tendai Rinos Mwanaka
When Escape Becomes the only Lover by Tendai R Mwanaka
ويَسهَرُ اللَّيلُ عَلَى شَفَتي...وَالغَمَام by Fethi Sassi
A Letter to the President by Mbizo Chirasha

104

This is not a poem by Richard Inya
Pressed flowers by John Eppel
Righteous Indignation by Jabulani Mzinyathi:
Blooming Cactus By Mikateko Mbambo
Rhythm of Life by Olivia Ngozi Osouha
Travellers Gather Dust and Lust by Gabriel Awuah Mainoo
Chitungwiza Mushamukuru: An Anthology from Zimbabwe's Biggest Ghetto Town by Tendai Rinos Mwanaka
Because Sadness is Beautiful? by Tanaka Chidora
Of Fresh Bloom and Smoke by Abigail George
Shades of Black by Edward Dzonze
Zimbolicious Poetry Anthology Vol 2 by Tendai R Mwanaka and Edward Dzonze
Best New African Poets 2015 Anthology by Tendai Rinos Mwanaka and Daniel Da Purificacao
Between Places by Tendai R Mwanaka
Best New African Poets 2020 Anthology by Tendai Rinos Mwanaka, Lorna Telma Zita and Balddine Moussa

Soon to be released

Denga reshiri yokunze kwenyika by Fethi Sassi

https://facebook.com/MwanakaMediaAndPublishing/

Printed in the United States
by Baker & Taylor Publisher Services